Text by **Benoît Delalandre** ⟶ Illustrations by **Benjamin Chaud** and Jé ⟶g Clapin

MY ATLAS OF THE HUMAN BODY

CONTENTS

INTRODUCTION

All Different - All Alike ⤏ 6-7

COMMUNICATING ⤏ 8-17

The Face ⤏ 9
Sight ⤏ 10
Hearing ⤏ 11
Smell ⤏ 12
Taste ⤏ 13
Touch ⤏ 14
Skin ⤏ 15
Emotions ⤏ 16-17

MOVING ⤏ 18-23

FOLDING CHART:
SKELETON AND MUSCLES ⤏ 19
The Bones ⤏ 20-21
Muscles ⤏ 22-23

EATING ⤏ 24-29

FOLDING CHART:
DIGESTIVE SYSTEM ⤏ 25
Digestion ⤏ 26
Teeth ⤏ 27
Food ⤏ 28-29

WASTE ⤏ 30-31

Waste ⤏ 31

BREATHING ⟶ 32-35

FOLDING CHART
RESPIRATORY AND CIRCULATORY SYSTEM ⟶ 33
Respiratory System ⟶ 34-35
Blood Circulation ⟶ 34-35

LEARNING ⟶ 36-43

FOLDING CHART:
NERVOUS SYSTEM ⟶ 37
The Brain ⟶ 38-39
Dangers ⟶ 40
Balance ⟶ 41
Fear ⟶ 42
Personality ⟶ 43

SLEEPING ⟶ 44-45

Sleep ⟶ 45

DEFENDING YOURSELF ⟶ 46-49

Defences ⟶ 47
Diseases ⟶ 48-49

GROWING ⟶ 50-57

Adolescence ⟶ 51
Sex ⟶ 52-53
Birth ⟶ 54-55
Growing Up ⟶ 56
Growing Old ⟶ 57

BODY FACTS ⟶ 58-59
BODY WORDS ⟶ 60-61
INDEX ⟶ 62

ALL DIFFERENT

We are all different. Some of us are tall. Others are short. Some are large while others are thin. Some of us have straight hair. Others have curly hair. Some of us have wide noses. Others have snub noses. Our eyes can be green, blue, black or brown. Some people are curious. Some are lazy. Some are greedy. You might be good at art or a champion at sport. Some of us love school, while others don't.

Each of us has a different **voice**.

Our **eyes** are unique (from close up, the iris in each eye forms a very complicated pattern).

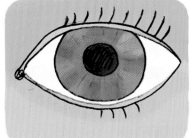

Everyone has a different **handwriting**.

Everyone has different **fingerprints** (fingerprints are the labyrinth patterns on the pads of your fingers).

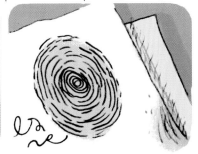

And each personality is unique: our **thoughts**, our **dreams**,

the way we **dress**,

go **downstairs**...

You are the only one living **your own special life**.

ALL ALIKE

In some ways, we are all alike. We are born from a father and mother. We like to play, eat well, laugh and sing. We don't like to be sad, to cry or feel unwell . We all want to be loved and have a happy life.

Whatever colour we are, we all have the same ancestors: the first homo sapiens. The children of homo sapiens spread out all over the Earth.

People who lived where the sun was very strong had dark skins. The hotter the sun, the darker the skin to protect the person from harmful rays.

Those who lived where the sun hardly ever shone had fair skins.

Today people of all colours live together all over the world.

A bag of bones, a few kilos of muscle and some organs inside us, all wrapped in a protective skin. We are all put together in the same way.

COMMUNICATING

THE FACE
Your face has holes in it, through which the world around you can get in.

Your face shows what is going on inside you. It expresses your **feelings**. It's difficult to hide them.

You are **frightened**: your eyes grow wide, your mouth opens, you put your head back.

You are **disgusted**: you wrinkle your nose, the corners of your mouth droop, your eyes narrow.

You are **angry**: you clench your teeth, your eyebrows frown, your face turns red.

You are **happy**: you smile, your eyes crinkle.

The **bones** of your face give it shape.

Above your face, your **hair** is a cushion, a sunshade and a hat.

The hair on your head consists of individual hairs, which grow from a **root**. These hairs keep falling out and growing again.

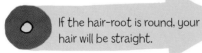

If the hair-root is round, your hair will be straight.

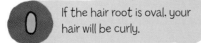

If the hair root is oval, your hair will be curly.

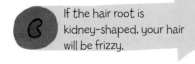

If the hair root is kidney-shaped, your hair will be frizzy.

Your **nose and ears** are not made of bone. They are supple cartilage. Otherwise they would often get broken.

SIGHT-HEARING-SMELL-TASTE-TOUCH
We have FIVE SENSES which tell us about the world around us.

Your **EYES** are for seeing, and also for crying or winking.

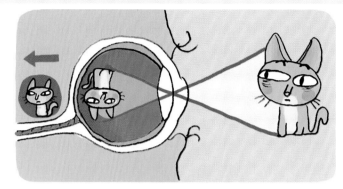

Light enters your eye through a little hole (the pupil) and lights up the back of your eye (the retina). The retina sends the information to your brain.

iris

You have to wait awhile to be able to see **in the dark**. The coloured part of the eye, the iris, is a ring of muscles. When it is dark, these muscles contract, so that the pupil grows bigger and more light can get through it. Then you can see better. But that takes a little while.

pupil

WHY DO YOU HAVE RED EYES IN A PHOTO?
The little red circle is the retina, lit by the flash.

Your eyes are producing **tears** all the time. They do not flow down your cheeks but disappear through a little hole in the corner of your eye and end up in the nose. That is why your nose gets snuffly when you cry.

Two eyes are better than one.
The two eyes side-by-side on your face tell you how far away the object you are looking at is.

HOW ABOUT ANIMALS?
A chicken has eyes on the sides of her head and can look out for danger all round. The fox has eyes in front. He knows exactly how far away the chicken is, to be able to pounce on her.

Your **eyelashes** act as a barrier to dust. As soon as anything touches them, they shut automatically.

Your **eyebrows** keep the sweat from your brow from running into your eyes.

Your EARS
are for hearing and also
for wearing earrings or
a hat.
Hearing is useful for
communicating with others.

The ear is shell-shaped to pick up **sounds** better. Sounds go right into the back of the ear, where the skin is tightly stretched (the tympanum or eardrum) and vibrates like a drum. A nerve carries the information to the brain.

WHY TWO EARS?
To know where the sound is coming from. If you hear it louder with your left ear, that means the sound is on the left. If you hear it just as well with both ears, that means the sound is in front or behind you.

If you have **sticking-out ears**, you can hear the sounds in front of you better.

The yellow wax in your ears is called **cerumen**. It greases the eardrum to keep it supple.

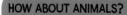

Earache (otitis): a microbe has got into the back of the ear behind the eardrum. It is red and swollen and hurts a lot. But earache often clears up by itself.

HOW ABOUT ANIMALS?
A cat can wiggle its ears separately in all directions.

Your NOSE
is for smelling but also for blowing, or for wearing glasses.

At the back of the nose there is a big cavity whose sides are lined with smell-sensors. The **smells** that enter the nose on the air are analysed and the information is sent to the brain.

WHY ARE YOUR NOSTRILS UNDER YOUR NOSE?
Because if they were on top of it, they would fill up with everything that fell into them.

Smells can also come from your mouth. The smell of a strawberry passes from your mouth to your nose.

HOW ABOUT ANIMALS?
Their sense of smell makes them able to find food, but also to sniff out a hidden predator.

WHY DOES POO SMELL NASTY?
Because you've been told that it's dirty. A baby who has not been told this isn't at all bothered by his nappy's smell.

We remember smells very well. Memories of the smell of smoke, of food cooking or of your brother's socks and trainers can come back to you a long time afterwards.

Food has four different **flavours**: sweet, salty, acid and bitter. We taste them on different areas of the tongue.

bitter
acid
salty
sweet

Your MOUTH
is for tasting
but also for
kissing and
pulling faces.

Taste is a mixture of flavour and smell. When you say you love the taste of strawberries, you mean you love its sweet and acid flavour, but also its strawberry smell. You need your tongue but also your nose to get the full taste.

If you block your **nose** and someone puts a drop of strawberry juice on your tongue and then a drop of raspberry juice, you can't tell the difference. They are both sweet and acid.

HOW ABOUT ANIMALS?
A snake smells with its tongue. It picks up little scent 'bubbles' floating in the air and takes them into its mouth.

If you unblock your nose, the smell of strawberry or raspberry wafts into it and then you can really tell the difference.

Your **SKIN** is for touching but also for tickling or decorating.

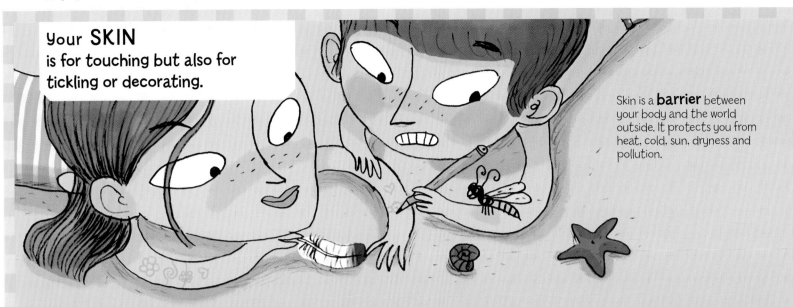

Skin is a **barrier** between your body and the world outside. It protects you from heat, cold, sun, dryness and pollution.

Your skin tells you about the **outside** world.

The wind **blowing**.

Heat from the fire.

Pain from a sting.

Shock from a hit.

Softness of a furry toy.

Your skin tells you what is going on **inside** you.

You are scared so your skin turns pale.

You are cold, so your skin goes red.

Under your skin there are thousands of little **receptors** which are sensitive to cold, heat, pressure or pain.

There are lots receptors on your fingertips.

There aren't many receptors on your bottom.

You are hot, so your skin sweats.

You are ill, so your skin comes out in spots.

Your skin **renews itself** all the time. You lose kilos of it every year.

HOW ABOUT ANIMALS?
A snake changes its skin all in one go. This is called sloughing its skin.

Sunburn

The sun's rays burn our skin. In order to protect itself it produces little grains of melanin, which repel the rays. As these are brown, our skin grows darker: it tans. Dark skins have more melanin than pale skins.

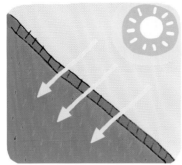
The sun's rays pierce the skin.

Melanin grains stop the rays.

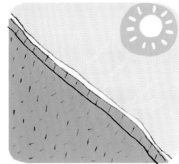
Sun creams stop the rays on the skin surface.

Melanin protects the skin but sometimes not fast enough. That is why you should always use sun cream.

Beauty spots

Beauty spots are little piles of melanin grains stuck together.

We are hairy animals.

Your hairs are longer on your head and shorter elsewhere. Under each hair there is a little muscle. When it is cold, the muscle contracts and the hair stands on end trying to trap warm air against the skin.
You have 'goose pimples'.

HOW ABOUT ANIMALS?
Your shoes are made of leather, which is cow skin. Shoes protect you from rain, cold and knocks.

HOW ABOUT ANIMALS?
A bird puffs out its feathers to trap warm air round itself.

Grease comes out through little holes called **pores**, to protect your skin and hair and keep them supple.

A baby in its mother's womb is covered in **down**.

EMOTIONS
Joy, fear, anger, sadness, disgust, surprise, shame, love: emotions colour our lives.

An emotion is when your body reacts to something from the outside. And it is your **brain** that controls it all.

For example, someone stands in front of you and tries to scare you. Your brain picks the appropriate emotion for the situation.

The most beautiful emotion is **love**. If the one you love loves you in return, then you are on top of the world. You feel special and very, very happy.

But look out! With love come other emotions, both good and bad: jealousy, envy, sadness, joy, shame...

People all over the world feel the same emotions.

We sometimes feel frightened of things we have heard or read.

MODESTY
We want to look nice when we walk along the street.

We cover up our bodies when we are around other people.

But at home or on the beach it may be different. Some families are very modest and others are not.

Tickling
makes you laugh if it's a game with someone you like. It's a way of giving pleasure.

Everyone likes presents and feels joy at receiving them.

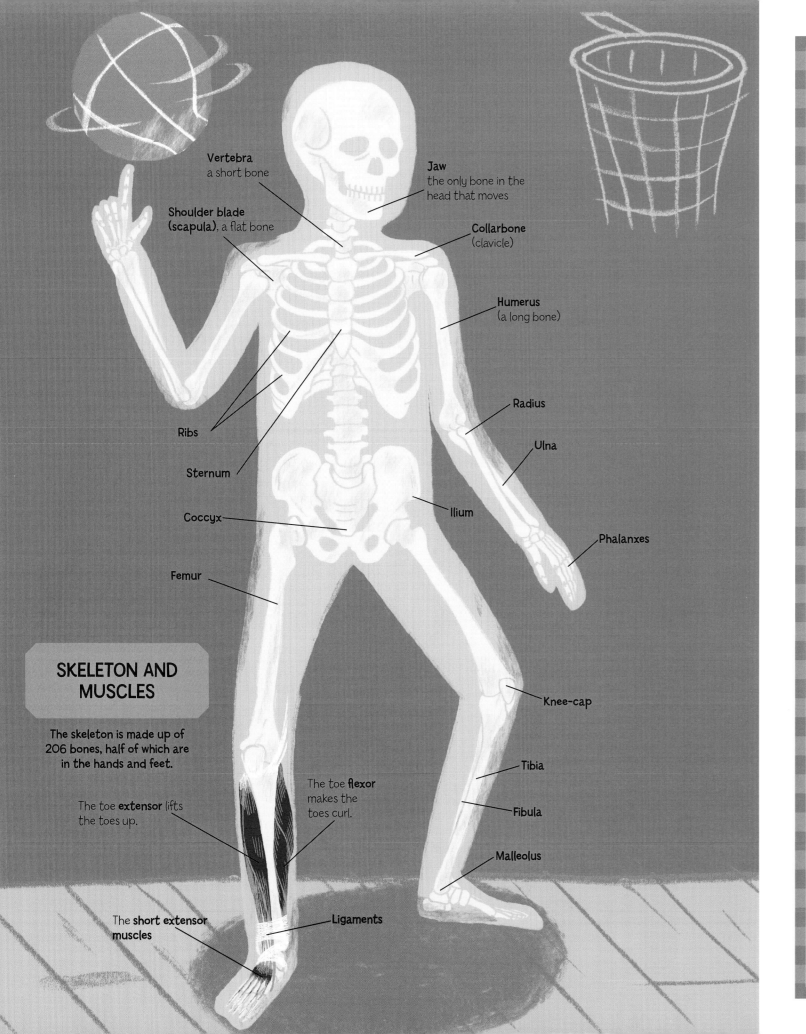

Vertebra
a short bone

Jaw
the only bone in the
head that moves

Shoulder blade
(scapula), a flat bone

Collarbone
(clavicle)

Humerus
(a long bone)

Ribs

Radius

Ulna

Sternum

Ilium

Coccyx

Phalanxes

Femur

Knee-cap

SKELETON AND MUSCLES

The skeleton is made up of
206 bones, half of which are
in the hands and feet.

Tibia

Fibula

The toe **extensor** lifts
the toes up.

The toe **flexor**
makes the
toes curl.

Malleolus

The **short extensor
muscles**

Ligaments

BONES
Your skeleton supports your body and makes it able to move. It also protects your internal organs.

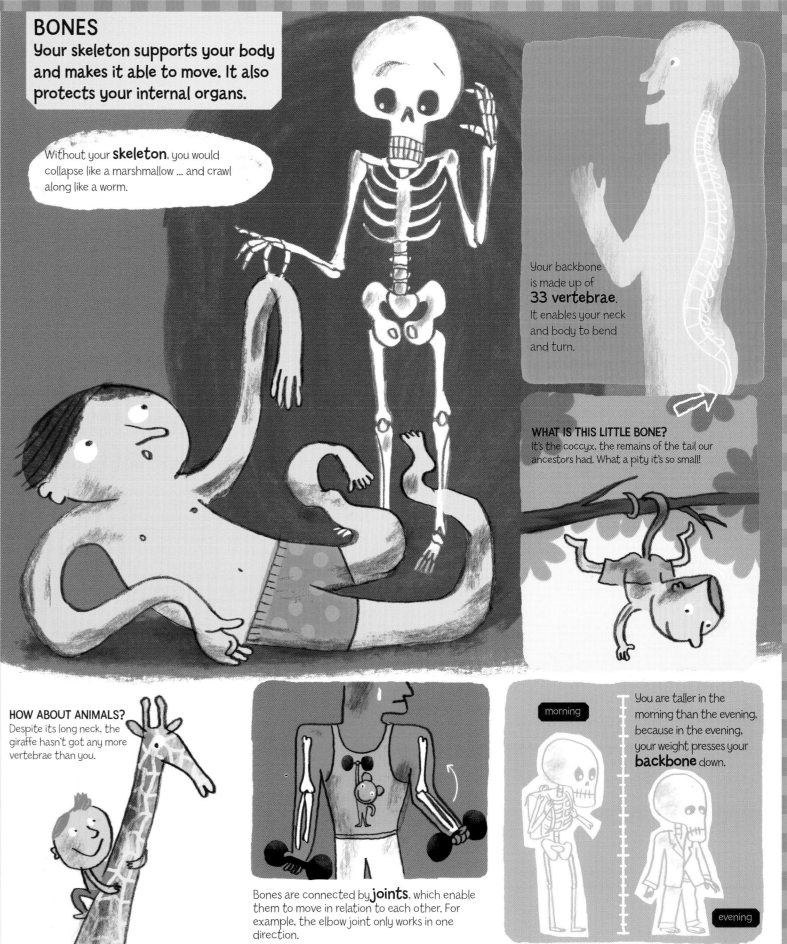

Without your **skeleton**, you would collapse like a marshmallow ... and crawl along like a worm.

Your backbone is made up of **33 vertebrae**. It enables your neck and body to bend and turn.

WHAT IS THIS LITTLE BONE?
It's the coccyx, the remains of the tail our ancestors had. What a pity it's so small!

HOW ABOUT ANIMALS?
Despite its long neck, the giraffe hasn't got any more vertebrae than you.

Bones are connected by **joints**, which enable them to move in relation to each other. For example, the elbow joint only works in one direction.

You are taller in the morning than the evening, because in the evening, your weight presses your **backbone** down.

morning

evening

Body language

I'm not scared of you.

I'm scared of him.

I don't know.

I've lost...

HOW ABOUT ANIMALS?
When you're angry you shout. You open your mouth wide to frighten your enemy like a rat facing a cat.

YOUR TRIBE
By dressing a certain way, walking a certain way, speaking a certain way, you show others who you are.

Each group has its own way of communicating.

VOICE
When air goes into your throat it makes two membranes vibrate. These are your vocal cords.

The air passing across the vocal cords makes them vibrate, like guitar strings. You can feel it by putting a finger on your throat.

When you whisper, your throat produces no sound. Your lips and tongue simply transform your breath into words.

Your tongue and lips move to turn the sounds your throat makes into words and songs.

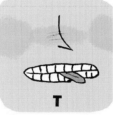 T
 O
 F

GETTING THE GIGGLES
First your face muscles open your mouth and crinkle your eyes. Then your stomach muscles push out air at 100 kilometres and hour. The vocal cords join in. Ha! ha! ha! Your neck and shoulders move, while your arms become limp. In the end the giggling slows down, you relax and feel calm and happy. Your muscles relax, including the bladder muscles. Laughing can make you wet yourself.

MOVING

Girls' bones are more slender. The pelvis is lower and wider (to hold a baby).

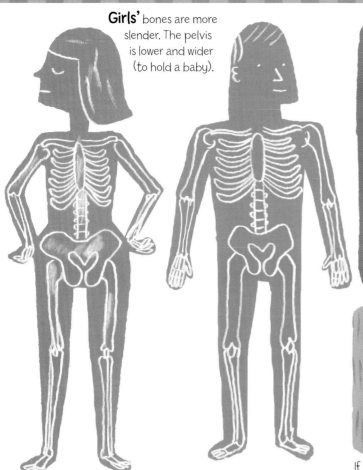

Bones also protect: the **cranium** protects your brain. Your ribs form a cage round your heart and lungs.

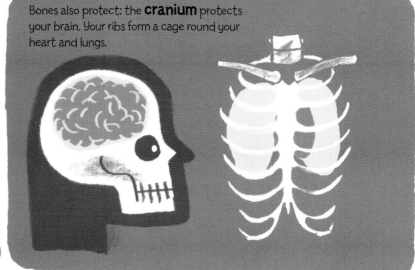

If your big toe is your longest toe, you have an **Egyptian** foot.

If your second toe is the longest, you have a **Greek** foot.

If all your toes are the same length, you have a **square** foot.

HOW ABOUT ANIMALS?
A crab has a skeleton instead of a skin.

To make them lighter, the bones are **hollow**. Bones have **marrow** inside them, which makes your blood.

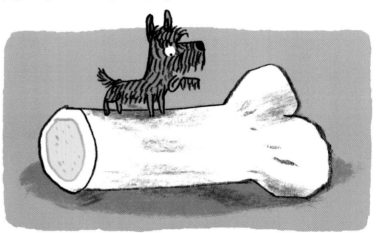

A BROKEN FINGER
To mend a broken finger, all you have to do is put the bone back in place and immobilise it with a splint or a plaster. After a short while it will mend all by itself.

MUSCLES
Muscles can only do one thing: contract.

You have **600** muscles to obey you. Some of them don't move until you **order** them to.

Other muscles work of their **own accord**. Your stomach contracts because it is hungry.

Just to smile you use **17** muscles.

To laugh you have to add another **15**: for voice, breathing and the stomach muscles.

You need **20** muscles to pull this face: eyebrow, eye, nose and tongue muscles.

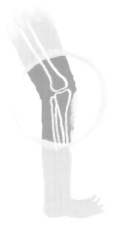

Joints
When a muscle contracts it pulls the bones, so that they move around the joint. Muscles are attached to the bones by thick tendons.

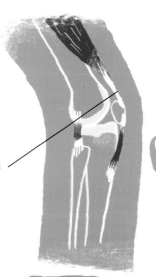

Certain muscles are **opposite** pairs. When one contracts, the other relaxes.

Winking
The fastest muscles are in the eyelids.

The **tongue** has 14 muscles which can move in all directions.

The harder a muscle works, the bigger it grows.

When astronauts are weightless, they do not have to bear their body's weight, so their muscles work very little. When they return to Earth, they find it hard to stand up.

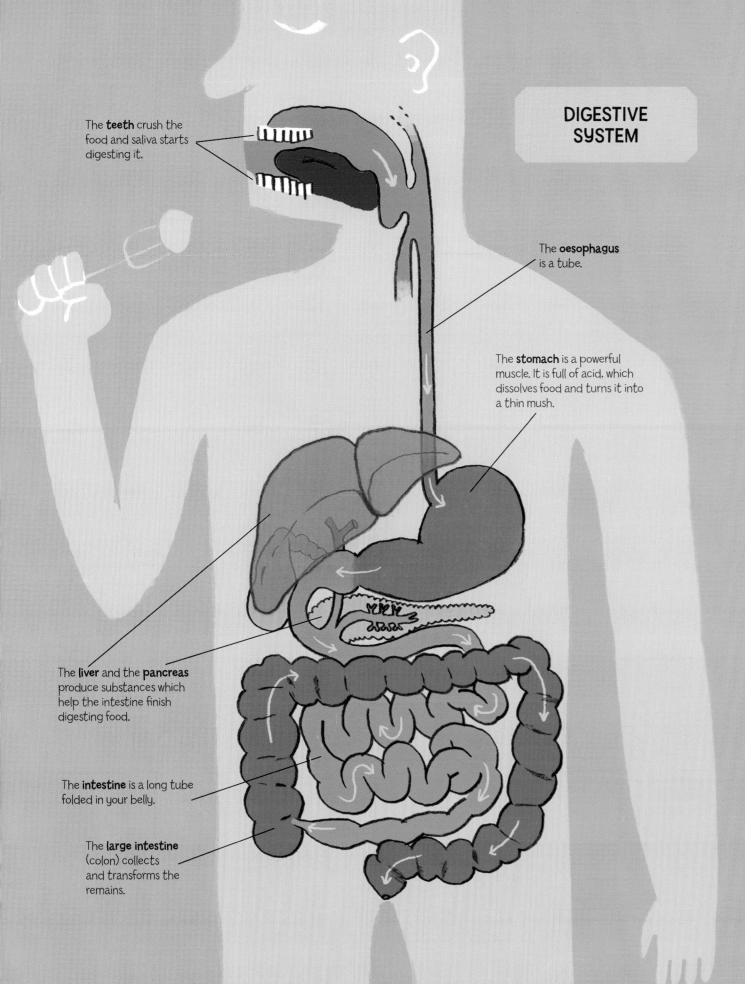

DIGESTIVE SYSTEM

The **teeth** crush the food and saliva starts digesting it.

The **oesophagus** is a tube.

The **stomach** is a powerful muscle. It is full of acid, which dissolves food and turns it into a thin mush.

The **liver** and the **pancreas** produce substances which help the intestine finish digesting food.

The **intestine** is a long tube folded in your belly.

The **large intestine** (colon) collects and transforms the remains.

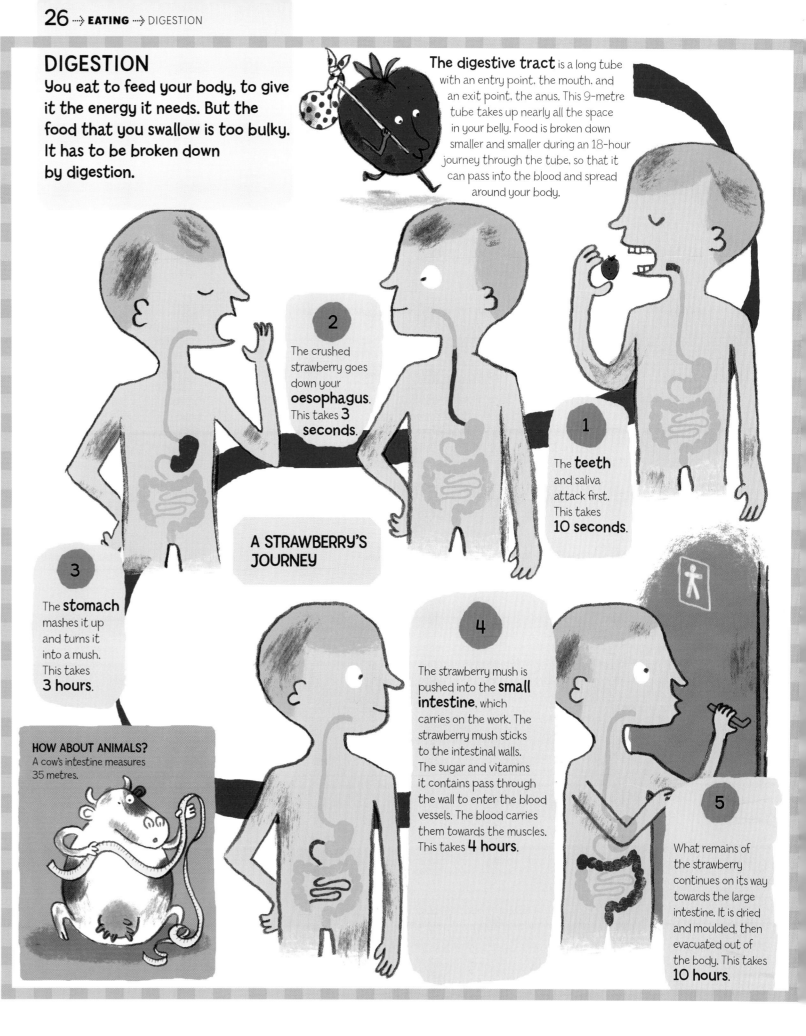

DIGESTION

You eat to feed your body, to give it the energy it needs. But the food that you swallow is too bulky. It has to be broken down by digestion.

The digestive tract is a long tube with an entry point, the mouth, and an exit point, the anus. This 9-metre tube takes up nearly all the space in your belly. Food is broken down smaller and smaller during an 18-hour journey through the tube, so that it can pass into the blood and spread around your body.

A STRAWBERRY'S JOURNEY

1 The **teeth** and saliva attack first. This takes **10 seconds**.

2 The crushed strawberry goes down your **oesophagus**. This takes **3 seconds**.

3 The **stomach** mashes it up and turns it into a mush. This takes **3 hours**.

4 The strawberry mush is pushed into the **small intestine**, which carries on the work. The strawberry mush sticks to the intestinal walls. The sugar and vitamins it contains pass through the wall to enter the blood vessels. The blood carries them towards the muscles. This takes **4 hours**.

5 What remains of the strawberry continues on its way towards the large intestine. It is dried and moulded, then evacuated out of the body. This takes **10 hours**.

HOW ABOUT ANIMALS?
A cow's intestine measures 35 metres.

ENGINE
Your muscles are your engine.

LIKE A CAR

PETROL
Your muscles need fuel, which is the sugar and oxygen carried to them by the blood. When they are working they consume this fuel and get hot ... like a car.

GREASE
For joints to work smoothly, they need to be kept greased, like an engine. The inner membrane secretes synovial fluid.

POLLUTION
When it is moving a car produces exhaust gas. When they are working your muscles produce waste. If they work too hard, your blood has no time to get rid of it all and the waste products pile up. That hurts. You feel stiff.

Before strenuous exercise, you have to warm up to give the blood time to bring the fuel.

Before and after exercise, you should drink and stretch to help eliminate the waste products.

A SPRAIN
You twist your ankle. Your ligaments are stretched or even torn. The doctor will bandage your ankle or put it in plaster to give the ligaments time to heal.

SUPER ANT!
If an ant was as big as you, it would be strong enough to carry your whole class in its arms.

EATING

Teeth

The incisors cut, the canines tear and the molars crush food.

A tooth is alive. It has blood and nerves in its root.
The tooth is covered with very hard enamel to protect it.
The adult tooth is tiny at first, then it pushes the milk tooth out.

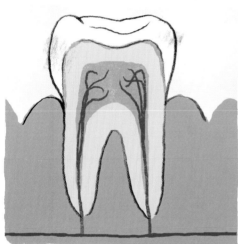

During your lifetime, you will produce enough **saliva** to fill a swimming pool.

HOW ABOUT ANIMALS?

Elephants have only 4 molar teeth. As they eat all the time they use them a lot. So these teeth are renewed 6 times during their lives.

Needing air

Muscles need oxygen to transform sugar into pure energy. Oxygen is brought into the body by breathing. Eating and breathing go together.

WHY DOES MY STOMACH MAKE SO MUCH NOISE?

Your stomach doesn't like to be empty. So it takes in air and gurgles.

FOOD
Food contains sugar which gives energy.

The sugar in sweets, fizzy drinks or cakes, passes into the digestive tract very quickly and immediately reaches the muscles.
This is called **fast sugar**. So if you eat sweets for an afternoon snack, you will only have energy for an hour.

Pasta, rice or bread do not taste sweet, but they also contain a lot of sugar. But this kind takes longer to digest.
It is called **slow sugar**. So if you eat bread for your afternoon snack, you will last till dinner time.

Food also contains:

Fats to build up extra supplies of energy.

Proteins to build your body and repair it.

1 kg of strawberries gives you enough energy to::

Watch **3 films on television**.

Roller-skate for **half an hour**.

Vegetables and fruit contain **fibre** which is not nourishing but helps with digestion.

Listen to your teacher for **2 hours**.

Run fast for **20 minutes**.

The sugars and fats you eat which your body does not use are stored in the form of **fat**.

If you start getting fat you should try to eat less fatty or sugary food. You should also make an effort to burn off this useless fat through exercise.

HOW ABOUT ANIMALS?
The seal needs its thick layer of fat to protect it from the cold.

UPSETS

Being sick
If something you have eaten is too big, or has gone bad, and your stomach does not like it, it gets rid of it by throwing it up. You are sick.

Diarrhoea
If your intestine does not like it, it gets rid of it downwards. You have diarrhoea.

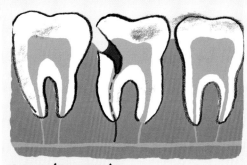

Caries (Cavities)
Microbes feed on food stuck between your teeth, producing an acid that destroys the tooth's enamel. Then the acid digs deeper till it touches your nerve. Ouch!

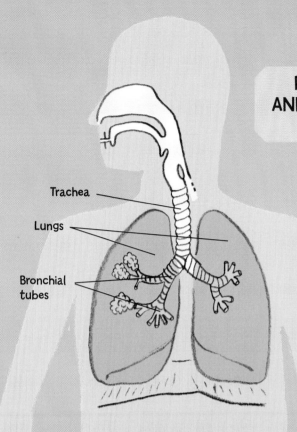

RESPIRATORY AND CIRCULATORY SYSTEMS

Trachea

Lungs

Bronchial tubes

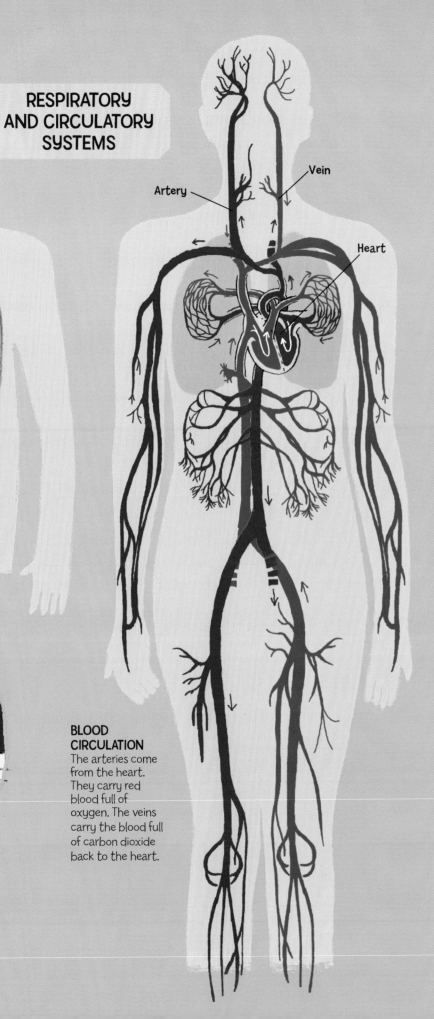

Artery

Vein

Heart

RESPIRATORY SYSTEM
Air goes in through your nose and mouth, down into the trachea and then reaches your **bronchial tubes**, which branch out into smaller and smaller branches until they come to the **alveoli**.

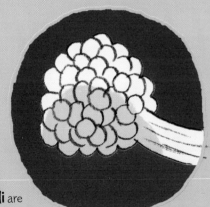

The **alveoli** are little balls whose walls are covered with blood vessels.

BLOOD CIRCULATION
The arteries come from the heart. They carry red blood full of oxygen. The veins carry the blood full of carbon dioxide back to the heart.

Breathing means filling your lungs with air. The air contains oxygen which the body must have.

To transform sugar into energy, the body needs oxygen. During the course of this the body expels carbon dioxide.

Sugar + oxygen = energy + carbon dioxide.

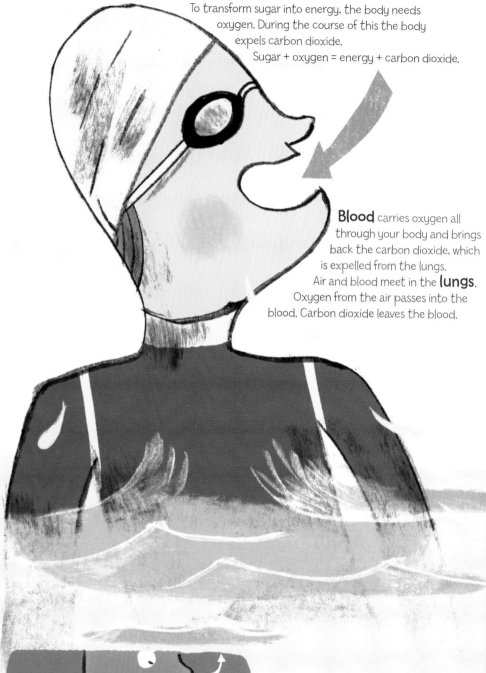

Blood carries oxygen all through your body and brings back the carbon dioxide, which is expelled from the lungs. Air and blood meet in the **lungs**. Oxygen from the air passes into the blood. Carbon dioxide leaves the blood.

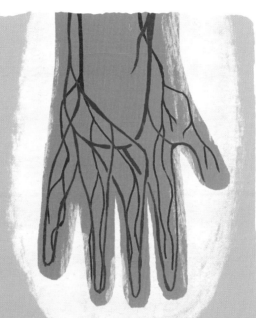

The tubes which carry the blood are called **blood vessels**. Those running from the heart – the arteries (shown in red) – distribute blood full of oxygen and nutriments all over the body. Those returning to the heart – the veins (shown in blue) – carry away the blood full of carbon dioxide and waste products.

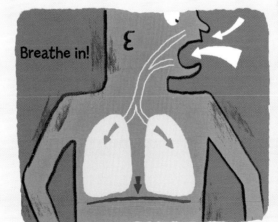

Breathe in!

Breathe out!

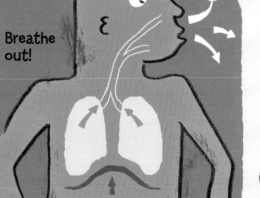

HOW ABOUT ANIMALS?
Fish don't have lungs. They have gills which absorb oxygen from the water.

THE DIAPHRAGM is a flat muscle situated under the lungs. It fills and empties the lungs with the help of the rib muscles.

Pee

The body produces waste, which is carried by the blood. To get rid of the waste, the blood flows through the kidneys, which clean it. The waste matter mixed with water becomes pee. It flows into the bladder where it waits for a while. When the bladder gets full, it sends a message to your brain. Quick, pee!

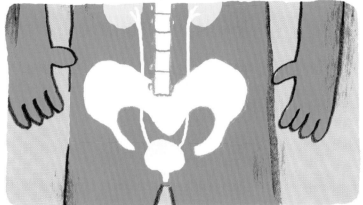

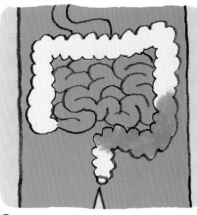

Poo

This comes from the food leftovers your body can't use. Your large intestine harbours millions of microbes which consume some of the leftovers. The rest are eliminated.

Gas

While they are feeding, the microbes in your intestine produce gas. When too much builds up it has to be evacuated.

HOW ABOUT ANIMALS?

Like most hairy animals, dogs do not sweat. So to cool their bodies down when they get hot, they leave their mouths open with their tongues hanging out. The water that evaporates in their mouths cool them down.

Sweat

When you are too hot you sweat. As it evaporates sweat cools you down. It takes the opportunity to evacuate some waste products from your body. That is why it does not smell nice.

The palms of your hands and the soles of your feet are the parts of your body that sweat the most. It is easy for hands which are in the fresh air. But shoes shut in the sweat and your feet paddle in it... to the delight of certain microbes which come along. They are what smell so nasty.

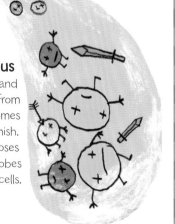

Bogey

It's a little heap of dirt. The air you breathe contains dust, smoke and microbes which are captured by your nose hairs.

Your nose produces a sticky liquid called **mucus**. The mixture of mucus and dirt forms a rather nasty little lump. That does not prevent some people from enjoying it. Yuk!

Green mucus

You've got a cold and the liquid running from your nose becomes thick and greenish. These are the corpses of the fighters: microbes against white cells.

BREATHING

UVULA AND EPIGLOTTIS

When you swallow a mouthful, the epiglottis shuts off the opening to the trachea. The uvula stops food getting into your nose. But if a small crumb gets past, there is an immediate reaction: you cough.

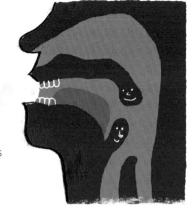
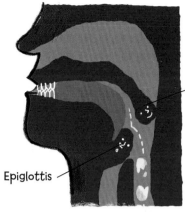

Uvula

Epiglottis

HOW ABOUT ANIMALS?
A lobster has green blood. Some snails have blue blood.

IN THE BLOOD
The red cells carry oxygen and carbon dioxide. The white cells attack microbes. The platelets plug up holes. When you hurt yourself, they form a crust which stops the blood flowing out.

Platelet

Red cell

White cell

THE HEART
Is a hollow muscle full of blood. It is as big as your fist. When it contracts, it pushes blood into the arteries. We say it beats.

When you make a big **effort**, your heart beats much more quickly to send more food and oxygen through your body, which really needs it.

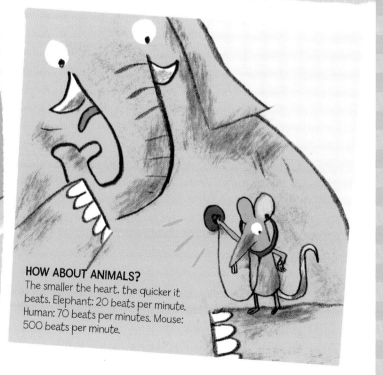

HOW ABOUT ANIMALS?
The smaller the heart, the quicker it beats. Elephant: 20 beats per minute. Human: 70 beats per minutes. Mouse: 500 beats per minute.

LEARNING

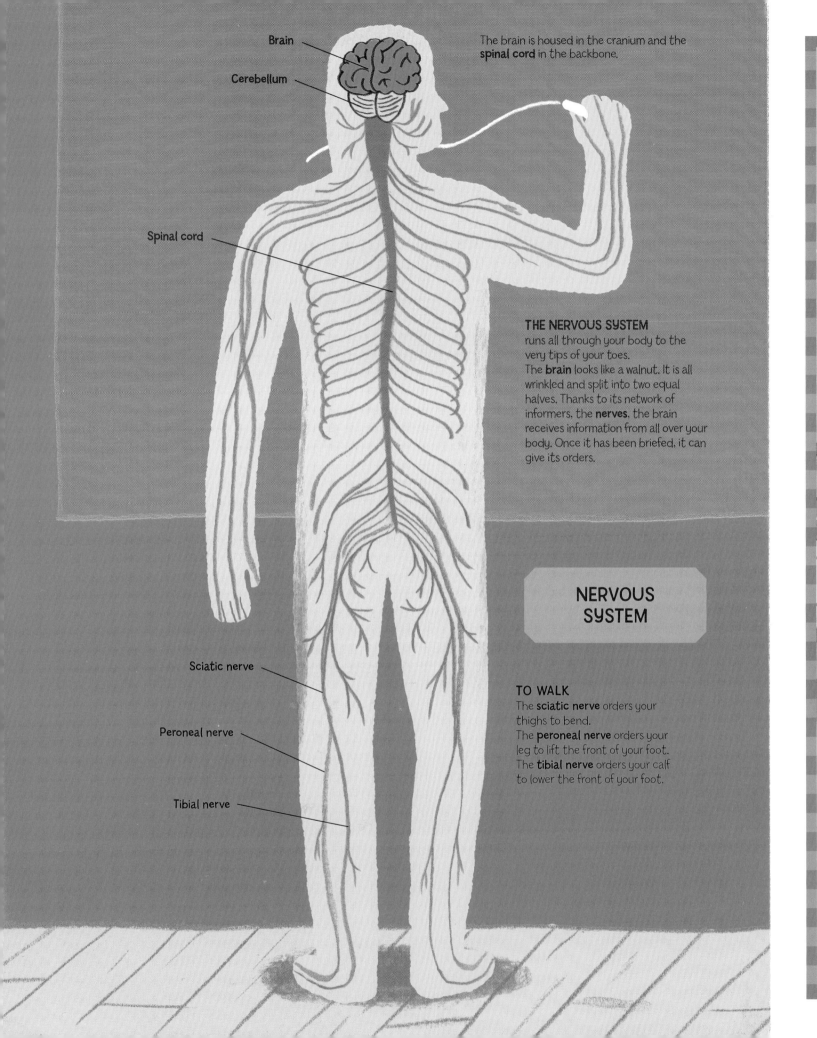

The brain is housed in the cranium and the **spinal cord** in the backbone.

Brain

Cerebellum

Spinal cord

THE NERVOUS SYSTEM
runs all through your body to the very tips of your toes.
The **brain** looks like a walnut. It is all wrinkled and split into two equal halves. Thanks to its network of informers, the **nerves**, the brain receives information from all over your body. Once it has been briefed, it can give its orders.

NERVOUS SYSTEM

TO WALK
The **sciatic nerve** orders your thighs to bend.
The **peroneal nerve** orders your leg to lift the front of your foot.
The **tibial nerve** orders your calf to lower the front of your foot.

Sciatic nerve

Peroneal nerve

Tibial nerve

THE BRAIN
The brain is the organ of thought, intelligence, memory and imagination. But it also controls the body. It takes all the decisions. It is the Big Boss!

The brain is capable of doing lots of things at the same time. For example, at this moment: you are reading, recognising letters, words, the meaning of sentences. You are sitting down with the help of a good number of muscles. Perhaps you are scratching your head, or chewing gum. You smell the book's smell, or the smell of the cake cooking in the kitchen. And of course, you are staying alive: you are breathing, digesting your last meal, your heart is beating and your hair is growing.

Luckily, most of the time your brain gets on without you. You tell your body to walk, but you don't have to worry about the 200 muscles needed to take just one step.

Under your skin you have **nerves** that are sensitive to heat, cold, pain and pressure. An order runs through the nerve like an electric current. If a nerve was cut, the order could not be delivered.

A baby's brain does not yet know how to control all its muscles very well.

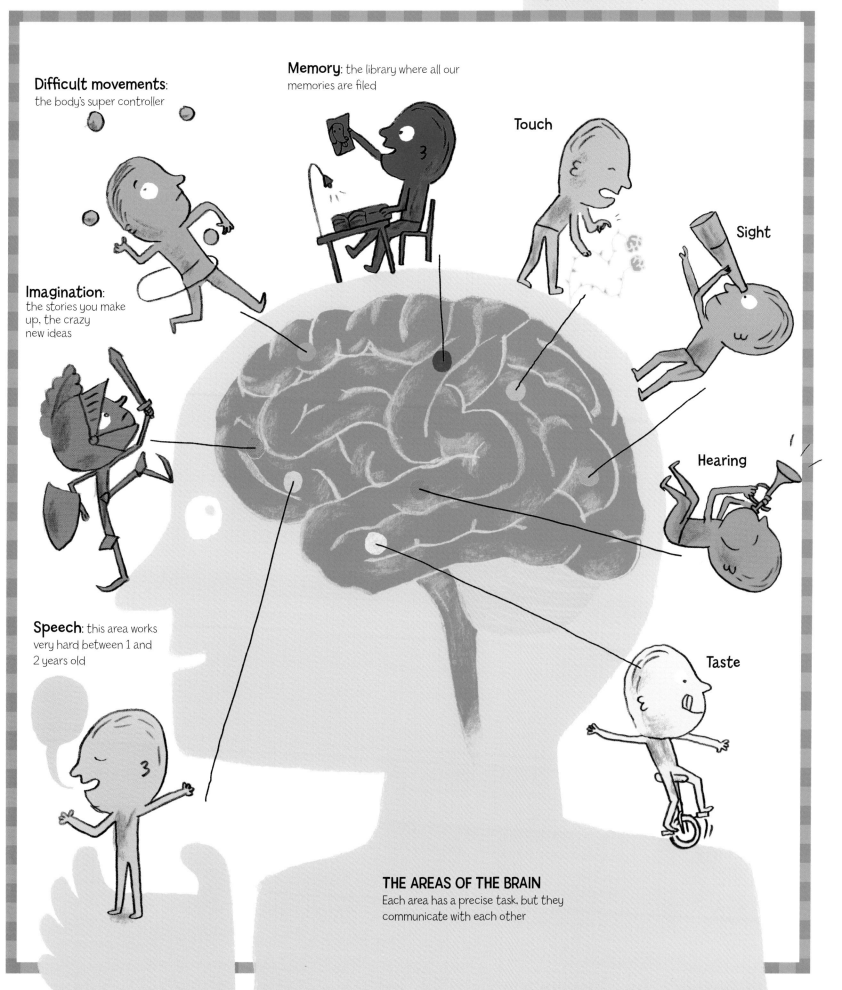

Difficult movements: the body's super controller

Memory: the library where all our memories are filed

Touch

Sight

Imagination: the stories you make up, the crazy new ideas

Hearing

Speech: this area works very hard between 1 and 2 years old

Taste

THE AREAS OF THE BRAIN
Each area has a precise task, but they communicate with each other

LOOK OUT!
The spinal cord is what reacts fastest to danger. It controls the reflexes.

The bath is **burning hot.**

The **nerves** in your foot detect pain and feel the heat.

The information is carried to the **spinal cord.** It immediately gives the order to take your foot out of the hot water.

The order is carried down to the foot muscles by the **motor nerves.**
The muscles pull the foot out of the water.

Then all the information is carried to the **brain,** which analyses the situation: the bath water is too hot!

The brain takes a decision and sends out its orders. Your arm and hand muscles turn on the cold water tap.

Danger's over! The whole thing has taken just a few seconds.

HOW ABOUT ANIMALS?
These chicks are hungry. They are waiting impatiently for their parents to come back. Suddenly a shadow blocks the light from outside. Immediately the three little yellow beaks open wide. They have reacted to the light change.

To keep your **balance** your brain has to keep calculating and giving orders to your whole body: your belly, back, bottom, arms, neck, feet.

BALANCE
If we were lizards it would be easy to balance on four legs, but we have to balance on two legs.

The brain calculates the body's balance by using a **sensor** deep inside your ear.

When you spin round for a long time, your sensor gets confused. When you stop spinning you feel **giddy**, because your sensor needs a little time to stabilise.

WHAT ARE YOUR TOES FOR?
As well as knocking on the end of the bed, your toes are very useful for keeping your balance.

FEAR
Your body and mind need to be prepared for danger in case something unexpected or bad happens.

Action stations! Your brain gives the alarm signal. Your **heart beats** much faster.

You **turn pale**, as your blood retreats from your skin to go to your muscles and brain (to concentrate and act swiftly and surely). You breathe more quickly (you need lots of oxygen). You sweat (your muscles will grow hot).

You feel alert
You have the energy ready to fight.

YOU ARE VERY STRONG!
You only have to display all this fighting energy to frighten your enemy away.

We all see the world in **our own way**.
A dog goes by.

Mary wants to stroke it.

Luke finds it ugly.

Joe is scared of it.

YOUR PERSONALITY
You have your qualities and shortcomings, your strengths and weaknesses. Your personality is unique like your body.

You are **unique** in the world. Your thoughts are your own. You have your own feelings and way of looking at the world. You are the only one to know your own private world, which you can escape into when you day dream.

Anne is scared of spiders. She sings well. She likes cherry sweets. She wants to be a singer.

Caroline is a chatterbox. She likes team sports. She is very ticklish. She wants to be a chef.

Peter likes to read books. He also likes climbing trees. He hates vegetables.

How about you? Do you like spiders or vegetables?

SLEEPING

At night when you are asleep, your body rests and repairs itself. After the day's noise and excitement, your brain can sort out your new experiences and arrange them in your memory.

You have two different kinds of sleep. First you sleep calmly, deeply and still. Your body is resting. This is called "Non-REM sleep."

Then suddenly your eyes start moving about in all directions, you breathe more deeply. You toss and turn. You dream. This is the period of "REM (Rapid Eye-Movement) sleep."

You go **in and out** of both kinds of sleep all night long.

To **dream**, your brain picks up moments you have just experienced, adds old memories, things you'd like to forget or have not understood. It mixes all these together with a lot of imagination. So often dream stories are strange.

In your dream your brain lives through a terrific adventure. Just as in the daytime, it sends messages to your muscles. Fortunately, your spinal cord blocks them.

A **nightmare** gives you the chance to relive situations that frighten you so that you can get the better of them. A nightmare also gives you the chance to experience forbidden things.

You grow while you are asleep, especially at the beginning of the night. That is why you need to go to bed early.

YAWNING
When you are tired or bored, you breathe more slowly. Your brain, which has got short of oxygen, orders you to yawn. That makes you open your mouth wide to take in a good mouthful of air.

DEFENDING YOURSELF

A COLD

The lining of your nose is irritated, so your body sends water to tend it. Your nose **runs**.

You **sneeze** to clear your nose. Atishoo!
You send out 5000 drops at 120 km per hour.

You **cough** to clear your throat.

MICROBES

Microbes are everywhere. They try to get into the fortress. It has gates that need guarding: your mouth, nose, ears, eyes or wounds.

Your body is like a fortress: its ramparts are your skin and its defenders are the white blood cells.

WHITE CELLS

But you are well equipped to defend yourself against these invaders. Your army of white cells is ready to fight.

The white cell swallows the microbe, then digests it. But sometimes the microbes win. Then you have to treat yourself with medicine.

VACCINATION

A few weakened microbes of a serious disease are injected into your body. Your white cells immediately produce new weapons to destroy them: **antibodies**. The white cells will keep these new weapons, so if the day comes when the real, unweakened microbes attack, the white cells will massacre them.

HIGH TEMPERATURE

The flu virus does not like heat, so to defend itself your body raises its temperature.

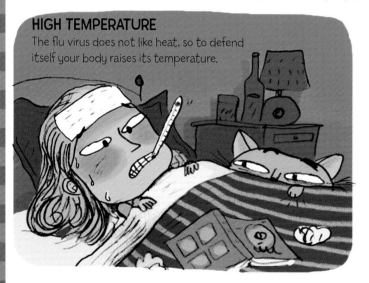

The flu virus does not like sun rays either, so you don't usually get flu in the summer.

The normal **temperature** of your body is 37°C.

Below 36°C or above 41°C makes you feel awful.

ALLERGY

Some people have strong reactions to flower pollen, pollution, house dust or cat hairs. They cough, come out in spots or swell up and go red. The body thinks it is dealing with a very dangerous substance, so it reacts very violently. But it is wrong. It is an error in its defence system.

HOW ABOUT ANIMALS?
Birds can also catch a cold. Their nose runs, they cough and sneeze.

A GRAZE
A scab forms. Under the scab the skin repairs itself and heals.

Then the scab falls off and sometimes leaves a little scar.

BUMPS AND BRUISES

Your skin is elastic and absorbs knocks. But sometimes the shock is too great. The blood vessels in your skin burst. A little blood gets out and forms a bruise.

When there is only bone under the skin the leaked blood forms a bump.

If you could see the microbes you collect on a simple walk through the town, you would hurry to wash your hands.

GROWING

WHAT'S GOING TO HAPPEN TO ME?
Don't worry. Your body know exactly what to do and when.

In some bodies these changes happen sooner than in other bodies.
Not every part of your body grows at the same rate. Sometimes your nose or your legs grow longer before anything else.

Everyone gets some little **annoyances**: spots, bad temper, feeling misunderstood.

The **smell** of your body will change: as if someone else had been wearing your clothes.

Girls and **boys** begin to be interested in each other.

HOW ABOUT ANIMALS?
Among many animals when the young males become adult, they are driven out of the group.

ADOLESCENCE
When you are 10-12, your body will gradually change into an adult body capable of producing children.

Hairs grow which are the colour of the hair on your head.

GIRLS
Grow breasts. Your body shape changes. Your ovaries begin producing ova. You get your first period.

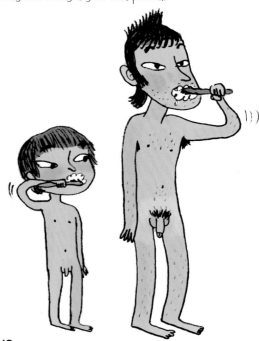

BOYS
Your penis and testicles grow. Hair grows under your arms, around your genitals and on your face. Your voice changes and becomes deeper. Your testicles begin producing spermatozoa.

SEX AND BABIES
A boy's sexual organs are different from a girl's, but they are made to fit together.

A **girl's** sexual organs are hidden in her lower belly. Her ovaries make ova. The baby will grow in her womb. It will be born through her vagina.

A **boy's** sexual organs are all on the outside: penis and testicles. The testicles make spermatozoa.

Penis

Testicle

WHY ARE TESTICLES OUTSIDE THE BODY?
Because they would be too hot inside the body at 37°C.

HOW ABOUT ANIMALS?
All these aphids are female. When she is born, each aphid already has all her future offspring inside herself. They are perfect copies of their mother. That is why aphids can reproduce very quickly.

Womb

Ovary

Vagina

Just once a month the girl's ovaries inside her produce an ovum. Every day a boy produces millions of spermatozoa in his testicles. When a spermatozoon meets an ovum they join together to form an egg. The egg will become a baby.

MAKING A BABY

1. When they make love, the boy and girl hug each other, they stroke and kiss each other. The boy's penis gently goes into the girl's vagina. It is a very pleasant moment for both of them.

2. Then the spermatozoa go out of the penis and make for the ovum. The fastest one enters the ovum and joins with it to form an egg. The egg will settle in the womb.

3. The ovum only lives three or four days. If the boy and girl make love during this time, an egg can form. This means the girl becomes pregnant. If they make love when there is no ovum there, the spermatozoa remain alone, so there is no egg and no baby.

Periods

Every month the womb produces a blood-swollen, cosy nest for the egg. If there is no egg, this nest is expelled. Then the girl loses a little blood through her vagina. This is a period. It lasts for a few days. Sometimes it can make you feel out of sorts.

To make love without having a baby

One way to stop the spermatozoa reaching the ovum is to cover the penis with a condom (like the finger of a rubber glove). The girl can also stop her ovaries producing an ovum by taking the contraceptive pill.

A BABY
The little egg will take nine months to become a baby.

The egg will grow quietly in its mother's womb, where it will be kept warm and fed and protected in a liquid bubble.

At **1 week** Baby is like a tiny raspberry.

At **7 weeks** Baby is like a tadpole with a tail. But its heart is already beating!

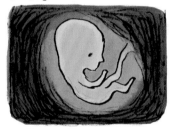

At **3 months** Baby is a miniature baby the size of a lollipop.

At **4 months** Baby moves, stretches and rolls about.

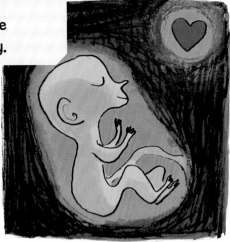

At **5 months** Baby is kicking hard. Baby can hear noises from outside, the boom-boom of Mother's heart and her stomach's glug-glug. Baby can suck its finger and yawn and swing about on the umbilical cord.

At **6 months** Baby's eyes open.

At **8 months**, Baby turns. It isn't easy as there isn't much room. Head first, baby is getting ready to be born.

When the time comes, the womb, which is a muscle, contracts and starts to push the baby out.

And suddenly, Baby has arrived! Head first. Baby gives its first cry. What a lot of intense new sensations: air in its lungs, smells, sounds. And all that space!

Amazing! Then lying in Mother's arms Baby searches for her breast.

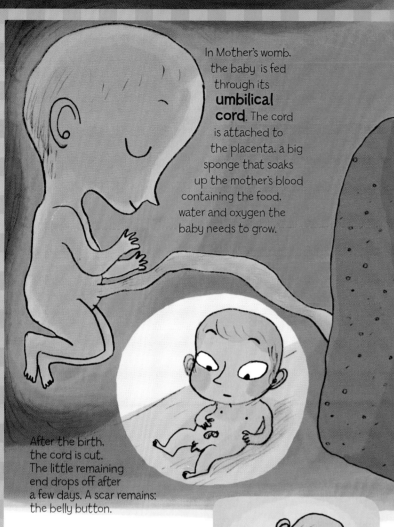

In Mother's womb, the baby is fed through its **umbilical cord**. The cord is attached to the placenta, a big sponge that soaks up the mother's blood containing the food, water and oxygen the baby needs to grow.

After the birth, the cord is cut. The little remaining end drops off after a few days. A scar remains: the belly button.

In its warm bubble Baby is aware of many things.

It sees ... day and night, strong sunshine.

It hears ... the sounds in its mother's belly, its father's voice, a barking dog.

It touches ... its daddy.

It tastes the liquid around it. If its mother likes spicy food, the liquid will taste spicy, and perhaps later the baby will like spicy food too.

DOES THE BABY PEE IN THE WOMB?
Yes.

HOW ABOUT ANIMALS?
Unlike human mothers, the mothers of all four-footed animals have wide pelvises so their young can stand up and gambol about almost as soon as they're born.

THE FIRST MONTHS
The baby feeds on milk. Best of all is its mother's milk although babies can be fed by bottle. Mother's milk contains everything the baby needs, and it is also the right temperature.

Babies often cry. It means: I'm hungry, I'm tired, my bottom stings. I want some attention.

GROWING UP
The world is open to you. You are going to live your life. Your life is unique.

At about **1 year old** you could walk.

At about age **1 and a half** you knew a few words and understood a lot more.

At about age **2**, you could run.

At about age **3**, you began to talk properly and could use your hands well.

At about age **4**, you loved to play. You had friends and enemies.

At about age **5**, you began to read.

At **5+**, you went to primary school.

Now everything will go faster and faster. You will keep on growing until you become an **adult**. You will have a job. You will fall in love. You will be happy and sad. Perhaps you will have children of your own. Life goes by so fast that you have to use every day well.

ONE DAY YOU ARE OLD
Your body has slowly grown old.

Your skin wrinkles. Your sight gets worse, especially your near sight. Your muscles weaken. Your voice changes. One day your body becomes worn out, so it stops.

Growing old is normal. It is part of life. That does not mean you can't still enjoy yourself, go on learning and falling in love.

We are living longer and longer because we eat better and take better care of ourselves. In the Middle Ages, few people lived longer than 40 or 50 years.

When you grow old your hair turns grey or white or you begin to lose it. Your eyebrows, nose hairs and eyelashes also turn white.

You can stay young at heart all your life.

Life on Earth never stops. Plants produce seeds which will become new plants. Animals have babies who will replace them. People have babies who will carry on their story. It's called the **Life Cycle**.

BODY FACTS

SPEED

HEIGHT

LENGTH

WEIGHT

AND MORE...

Nerves send messages to your brain at more than 360 km per hour.

Hair grows 1 cm per month. If you let it grow all your life and it did not fall out, it would be 10 m long when you were 80. You could make a splendid bun with that!

Your **brain** grows four times heavier during your first year of life.

During the day you blink your **eyelids** about 20,000 times.

When you **sneeze**, the air shoots out of your nose at about 160 km per hour.

The American man **Robert Wadlow** (1918-1940) measured 1.63 m at age 5; 1.83 at age 8; 2 m at age 11; 2.34 at age 15; 2.61 m at age 20; and 2.72 m at age 22, when he died.

The smallest bone in your body is the **stirrup**. It is in your ear. It measures about 3 mm. Your longest bone is the **femur**, your thigh bone, which measures about 50 cm.

Everyone **burps** about 15 times a day, sometimes without realising. In 1 year you burp (15 x 365) = 5475 times!

Your body contains 96,000 km of **blood vessels** - more than twice the Earth's circumference!

The American man Daniel Browning is able to **twist** his torso 180°. He is nicknamed 'Rubber Boy'!

You spend a third of your life (about 25 years) **asleep** and 5 years dreaming!

Many people eat about 100 g of **meat** per day. At age 10 a child has already eaten a whole pig. By age forty he will have eaten a whole cow.

You produce 15.000 litres of **pee** during your lifetime and use 100 km of toilet paper.

More than half the human body consists of **water**. No one can go without drinking for more than 2 days.

Our body has up to 1 million **hairs**.

3 kilos! That's the **skin** weight of a child aged 6! And if you could take it off like a coat. it would cover 1.5 square metres - the size of a large bath towel.

The **sciatic nerve** is the longest nerve. It controls the leg and foot muscles.

The **high jump** record was set in 1993 by the Cuban Javier Sotomayor who jumped 2.45 m.

The world's **smallest surviving baby**. born in the USA. weighed 284 grams. At 24 cms long she was the same size as a ballpoint pen.

When a child **writes**. the pen covers about 2 m per minute. After a year it will have covered more than 50 km!

The **blood** circulates in your body at a speed of 2 km per hour.

The world's **heaviest surviving baby**. born in Brazil, was twice the size of a normal six-month-old baby.

The Chinese woman **Zeng Jinlian** (1964-1982) measured 1.56 m at age 4, and 2.48 m at age 20.

In 1991 at the Tokyo Olympic Games. the American Mike Powell set a **long jump** record by jumping 8.95 m. If he had been on the Moon that day, he would have jumped 54 m. That is the length of a football pitch!

BODY WORDS

A

Antibiotic: A medicine that kills certain microbes such as bacteria.

C

Calcium: Calcium is necessary to make bones strong. It is found mainly is cheese and milk.

Carbohydrate: Carbohydrates give the body energy. They are found in bread, pasta, potatoes and other food.

Cell: A cell is the smallest element that goes to make up a living being. Humans are made up of millions of cells, which are different according to which organs they belong to: liver, muscle, blood cells...

Clotting: When blood clots (coagulates), it means it goes solid. Clotting stops a wound bleeding.

Colour blindness: People who are colour blind find it hard to see certain colours and tend to confuse green and red.

D

Doctor: Some doctors are General Practitioners and treat the whole body. Others specialise and treat

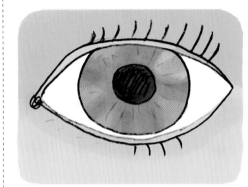

one or more parts. Ophthalmologists treat eyes. Paediatricians treat children. Dermatologists treat the skin.

E

Embryo: The name given to a baby in its mother's womb until it is 3 months old.

Epidermis: The skin's outer layer.

Eye-socket: The hole in your skull for the eye.

F

Foetus: The name given to the baby in the womb from 3 months until birth.

Freckles: Little packets of melanin which mainly appear on the pale skins of blond or red-haired people.

H

Hormones: Chemical substances circulating in the blood that give orders to certain organs in the body.

I

Infection: A mega-attack by microbes. If you have an infection somewhere, you often have a temperature.

K

Keratin: Material that hair and nails are made of.

Knee-cap: The flat bone protecting your knee.

L

Larynx: The part of your throat where your vocal cords are.

Lipids: Fats that store reserve energy. They are found in oil and butter.

P

Papillae: The tiny buds covering your tongue. They enable you to recognise a salty, sweet, bitter or acid taste.

Poo: The scientific word for it is faeces. Doing a poo is defecating.

Pregnancy: The nine month period when the mother carries the baby in her womb.

Protein: Meat, fish, eggs are rich in proteins. They are vital for growth.

Puberty: The change in the body at adolescence.

R

Ribcage: Set of bones that encloses the heart and lungs.

S

Scan: A scan makes it possible to see inside the body, for example a baby in the womb.

Sperm: The liquid emitted from the penis that contains the spermatozoa.

Stethoscope: An instrument used by doctors to listen to your breathing and heart beats.

T

Tonsils: Small organs at the back of your throat. Their job is to destroy passing microbes.

V

Virus: A tiny microbe responsible for colds or flu.

Vitamins: Contained in food, vitamins are very important to health and well-being.

Vulva: The name of a woman's external genital organs.

W

Willy: The scientific name for the willy is the penis.

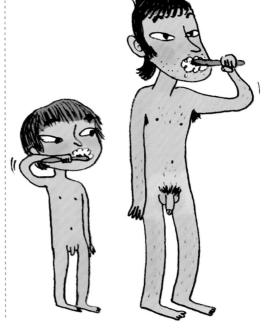

INDEX

A
Adolescence 51
Allergy 49
Antibiotic 60

B
Backbone 20, 37
Balance 41
Blood 33, 34, 35
Bones 9, 19, 20, 21
Brain 37, 38-9, 40 41

C
Calcium 60
Carbohydrate 60
Cell 60
Cerumen 11
Clotting 60

Colour blindness 60
Condom 53

D
Digestion 26, 27
Digestive tract 26
Diseases 48, 49
Doctor 61

E
Ear 11
Eardrum 11
Earache 11
Embryo 60
Emotion 16
Epidermis 60
Eyes 6, 10
Eye-socket 61

F
Fat 28, 29
Fingerprints 6
Foetus 60
Freckles 61

H
Hair 9
Hearing 11
Heart 33, 35
Hormones 60

I
Infection 60
Intestine 25, 26

J
Joints 22

K
Keratin 61
Knee-cap 61

L
Larynx 61
Lipid 61
Lung 34, 35

M
Melanin 15
Microbes 47
Muscle 19, 22, 23

N
Navel 55
Nerves 37, 38, 40
Nose 12

O
Oesophagus 25, 26
Ovary 52, 53
Ovum 52, 53
Oxygen 27, 34

P
Penis 52, 53, 61
Period 53
Pill 53
Placenta 55
Pregnancy 60
Proteins 28, 61
Puberty 61
Pupil 10

R
Red cells 35
Retina 10

S
Scan 60
Sex 52
Sight 10
Skeleton 19
Skin 14, 15
Sleep 45
Smell 12
Sperm 61
Spermatozoa 52, 53
Spinal cord 37, 40
Stethoscope 61
Stomach 25, 26
Sugar 28

T
Taste 13
Taste buds 61
Teeth 27
Testicle 52, 53
Touch 14
Tonsils 60

U
Umbilical cord 55
Uvula 35

V
Vagina 52, 53
Virus 61
Vocal cords 17
Voice 6, 17
Vulva 61

W
White cells 35, 47
Willy 61
Womb 52, 53, 54.

© Larousse 2008
21 rue du Montparnasse
75006 Paris, France
First published in Great Britain in 2008
by Tango Books Ltd
PO Box 32595, London W4 5YD
sales@tangobooks.co.uk
Tel: +44 20 8996 9970
www.tangobooks.co.uk

Translation by Translate-a-Book, Oxford UK
Translation © 2008 Tango Books Ltd

Edition: Marie-Claude Avignon
Direction editoriale: Françoise Vibert-Guigue
Direction de la publication: Isabelle Jeuge-Maynart
Direction artistique: Cédric Ramadier & Frédéric Houssin
Conception graphique: DOUBLE
Lecture-correction: Madeleine Biaujeaud
Fabrication: Nicolas Perrier